How to Become the Best Network Marketer Possible

By: Vanisha Alexander-Marshall

OVERVIEW

We will give you an overview of what we feel is the definition of a professional network marketer. We hope this system helps someone wanting to become a network marketer or already in the field a better idea of how to behave in the network marketing circuit and hopefully learn how to run a better, smarter, more efficient home based business. With the experiences we have gone through, we can show you the tools of what we feel are the right ways and wrong ways of being a network marketer.

DISCLAIMER

This is strictly based on personal experiences combined with research. We do not feel the experiences we have gone through will be the same experiences you will endure during your network marketing experience. Please be advised this is only based on personal experiences and research.

How to Become the Best Network Marketer Possible

By: Vanisha Alexander-Marshall

CHAPTERS

Chapter 1: What is Network Marketing?

Chapter 2: What Does Network Marketing Consists Of?

Chapter 3: The Advantages and Disadvantages of Network Marketing

Chapter 4: Network Marketing and Pyramid Schemes

Chapter 5: Being Professional in Network Marketing

Chapter 6: How to Handle Competition in Network Marketing

Chapter 7: What Can We Learn About Network Marketing?

Chapter 1

What Is Network Marketing?

Network marketing is defined as "a business model in which a distributor network is needed to build the business. Usually such businesses are also multilevel marketing in nature in that payouts occur at more than one level ("Network Marketing", Entrepreneur)." So what does that mean to the person entering the network marketing world for the very first time? It could mean a lot of things. It could mean just meeting a lot of people. It could mean being a referral for someone else that is trying to build their own business. However, it could be very confusing to someone that has never heard of network marketing. In a nutshell, network marketing is simply a world where companies have representatives or contractors that market their products or services. In return, that representative or contractor builds a business out of it. Simple enough? Great!

Network marketing can be a tricky process. Not every company are what they are cracked up to be. You have to do your research on these companies before you decide which company is best for you.

There are some key elements you need to know about network marketing. The first thing you would do is find the right company that fits your needs. Remember when you were pursuing your first job? Remember the first time you walked into the office and you were nervous about the new boss and the new people you were going to work with? Finding a network marketing company is the same thing. You want to make sure you find the right company that best fits you.

Next, find a company with a good track record. Do not jump into the first network marketing company and not know anything about them. Read about the company and lookup any information about the company such as the Better Business Bureau, Google, or Yahoo. Bottom line, do your homework on the company before you decide the right the company as your network marketing company of choice. Too many times we have seen people choose a company and then realize after the fact it is not what the company is all about and it becomes too little too late.

Next, find a company that you feel you can expand your career in the network marketing the best. When you are first introduced to the company, it is very important to get a feel of the atmosphere. See how the representatives that are introducing you and the other people to the company interact with each other. See how knowledgeable they are about the information they are presenting to you. Pay close attention to how the representatives are treating you and the other guests in the room. Remember, the other guests are also getting a feel of the company and are also deciding whether or not to join the company. Take notes! When exploring a network marketing opportunity, it is very important to bring a pen and notebook with you so you can take some valuable information down on the information that is being presented to you regarding the company, how you can grow in the company, and how you can have a successful network marketing business. The representatives that are presenting the information are trying to get a feel for you and the other guests as well and they are trying to see how well you will do on their team. These representatives are working very hard to get you and the other guests to join the company but more importantly, the question should be is whether this company is a good fit for you? Don't be afraid to ask questions. They should have the knowledge and ability to handle any questions that come their way regarding the presentation, the company, or anything. At the end of the day, it is about you making the right decision in your network marketing career and not them. Do not let them bully you into a decision that you will regret later.

Finally, find a company that has a great compensation plan that you can earn a great residual income. A lot was just said in the last sentence so let's break it down. First, let's define residual income. Residual income is defined simply as doing something one time and earning money for it for a lifetime. The best example that a lot of people in network marketing use to describe residual income is

Michael Jackson. He recorded the album "Thriller" back in 1982. Even in death, Michael Jackson's estate is still making money from the "Thriller" album, something he recorded one time over thirty years ago and his estate is still making money. The power of residual income is incredible yet powerful.

Now that we have defined residual income, now we can dive into the compensation plan. Many of the network marketing companies have different compensation plans for you to earn residual income. It is very important that you study their compensation plans and understand it.

We cannot stress how important it is to learn the company's compensation plan. The reason why we stress about the compensation plan is simply because these companies tend to promise you one thing but something else ends up happening and you end up not being paid in the timely fashion the company says it will do. For example, a lot of these companies will have grace periods in place before you earn your first commissions so beware of those grace periods. Make sure the company that you are researching spells out everything when it comes to their compensation plans and how and when they pay their representatives. Many companies do offer prepaid bank cards when you first get started with the company and some will not give you a bank card unless you have earned a certain amount of money. Others will offer direct deposit into your bank account when you earn your first commission money. It is imperative that you get all of these questions answered when it comes to the compensation plan because when the representatives talk about how a potential representative gets paid, they will start to fast talk through the compensation plan without taking the time to go through the plan thoroughly. A lot of the times, the representatives are just looking for people just to line their own pockets without caring about you or the guests they have invited to the presentation. Remember, in network marketing you are trying to build a business for yourself as well as the other representatives are trying to do the same thing. The question for you is whether or not the network marketing company you are scoping out is the right fit for you? Get all of those questions answered and make your final determination on the company you are researching.

Chapter 2

What Does Network Marketing Consist Of?

Once you have chosen the network marketing company that you will build your business with, you are probably wondering what to do next? I have chosen my company but where do I go from here? Well, let me tell you. Network marketing consists of these traits: start-up cost, flexible hours, recruiting, traveling, branding, and multi-level marketing (team building).

The most important thing to have is your representative that enrolled you in the company to help you build your network marketing business. The representative that helped you get started in your business is referred to as your up line. The name up line will be a name that you will hear in your network marketing career quite often. These are the people that have the knowledge of the company and they are the people that you can go to for help while you are building your business. The first thing you did when you got started in your business was pay a start-up or enrollment fee. This fee (or franchise fee) is paid so you can license the brand and the products and/or services the company offers. You are also able to use the company's name when you are marketing your business.

Remember, the business that you are marketing is also your "franchise" home based business.

When you are working your new business, your success will depend on the amount of hours that you put into your business. Just like any business whether it is network marketing or not, your success depends on the amount of hard work and the number of hours you put in to guarantee your success. However, do not expect success if you only put in 30 minutes every other day or 15 minutes once a week. If you put in one or two hours every day, you can expect some success. If you put in more than three hours a day, then you are looking at greater success. If you add up the hours, it is part time hours. Many people believe that when you first start out in network marketing that you have to quit your job to become a network marketer. This is simply not true. A vast majority of network marketers have full time jobs and work their home based businesses on a part time basis. However, the hard work and the allotted hours they dedicate to their business, some network marketers that become successful eventually quit their jobs and work their businesses full time. Again, it depends on the amount of time that you work your network marketing business.

Next, to expand your network marketing business, you will find yourself on several conference calls and webinars. The person that got you started in your home based business will put you in connection with these conference calls to help you grow your business. These conference calls can be very helpful not only in your business, but in your network marketing career. These conference calls are simply training calls that are hosted by your up lines and they train you on the products and services the company has and they train you on how to seek new business partners, how to pitch the products and services to new customers, and how to talk to different people (also called prospects). Be mindful of these conference calls. Do not get lost in the shuffle of these conference calls and know the difference between a good conference call and a bad conference call. A good conference call consists of good training with a good question and answer session and helping you grow your network marketing business. A bad conference call consists of bashing the company, bashing other up lines and representatives that are part of the company, and getting you involved in any company politics that becomes unnecessary and unprofessional. Some of these bad conference calls can trick you in to joining another company (also known as cross-recruiting).

Next, in growing your network marketing business, it will require you to travel. Most network marketing companies hold conferences and other events every year or several within the year which can help your network marketing business grow. These conferences and other events are a great way for you to network with other like-minded network marketers that are not only part of your company but also those that are successful in the company and have become the "heavy hitters" in the company. These "heavy hitters" are the people that you can learn from the most and they can show you how they became successful in the company and show you how you can have similar success in the company. However, you won't know unless you travel to these conferences and other events to grow and expand your business.

Next, in network marketing, you will grow your business by having people join your business. This is known is multi-level marketing. Multi-Level Marketing is defined as "a strategy that some direct sales companies use to encourage their existing distributors to recruit new distributors by paying the existing distributors a percentage of their recruits' sales. The recruits are known as a distributor's downline ("Multi-Level Marketing", Investopedia). Simply put, you become the representative and you're trying to recruit people for your home based business and you are looking for people that may be interested in starting their own home based business with the network marketing company that you are with and would like to become a representative for the company to be able to become a distributor to offer the product and/or services the company offers. Just like the representative that got you started in your network marketing business, you become the representative to help someone get started in their network marketing business. As time goes on, your business will continue to grow by continuing to help someone start their business with the company. In network marketing, this is called duplication. In order for your business to really be successful, you want your new representatives to duplicate what you did so their business is successful.

Finally, in network marketing, the most important thing is branding. Sure, you've gotten started with a network marketing company and you're growing your business but you must realize that in network marketing, it is your name that you are putting out there. It is your face that you are putting out there. It is about you and growing your business so it is very important that you grow your name, your brand, your business. Even though you are with a network marketing company, do not just put the name of the company as the forefront all of the time. The first thing people are going to remember with this company is you. Again, grow your name, yourself, grow your brand.

With branding will come an image change.

Your attitude will be different and your friends

and family will definitely notice a change. It is

all about branding yourself for your business.

A lot of people close to you will not understand

it but in the long run, it will pay off in your

business. Brand yourself!

Chapter 3

The Advantages and Disadvantages of Network Marketing

With any business that you begin whether it's in network marketing or not, there will be advantages and disadvantages that you will face. The advantages of network marketing consists of being your own boss, being able to spend more time with your family, being able to make an unlimited income, being able to work part-time, and being able to travel more with your family. Some of the other advantages of network marketing are becoming debt free, being able to set up college funds for your children and not having to ever worry about money again. The biggest advantage of network marketing is once again residual income as discussed in chapter two.

With the advantages comes the disadvantages of network marketing. The biggest disadvantage you will face in network marketing consists of being labeled as a pyramid scheme. It is by far the biggest hot button issue in network marketing any many people unfamiliar with the industry will immediately associate network marketing with a pyramid scheme. This subject will be discussed further in chapter four.

Another disadvantage of network marketing is the money earned depends on the number of hours and the amount of time you put in to work the business. The people from the outside will not understand it because they will believe that you are working too much and taking too much time away from your family. But understand with any business that you start, you will spend a lot of time away from those closet to you in order for your business to become successful. It is the same in network marketing. Understand that in network marketing, it is not going to come as easy as what some people may tell you. You will have your ups and downs and knowing the advantages and disadvantages of network

marketing are keys to your success.

Chapter 4

Network Marketing and Pyramid Schemes

The biggest challenge most network marketers will face is being compared to a pyramid scheme. A pyramid scheme is defined as "participants attempting to make money solely by recruiting new participants into the program with the promises of sky-high returns in a short period of time for doing nothing other than handing over your money and getting others to do the same. The fraudsters behind the pyramid scheme may go to great lengths to make the program look like a legitimate multi-level marketing program but despite their claims, the pyramid will collapse

("Pyramid Schemes", SEC.gov).

Unfortunately, this is a very common

problem in network marketing. If you really

think about it, pyramid schemes are very close

to being called Ponzi schemes. Many network

marketing companies are compared to

pyramid schemes and these companies have

been given a bad name.

But what many people do not realize

about pyramid schemes are that everyone are

involved in some type of pyramid. Think about

it for a minute. When you are on your job, that

job consists of a CEO, a president, a vice-president, managers, supervisors and blue and white collar employees. Everyone on that job fall under one of these categories. In Corporate America, this is known as an organizational chart. But when you look at the organizational chart on paper, doesn't the organizational chart look like a pyramid scheme? People outside of the network marketing world would never see it as such until you show them in a network marketing presentation that the job they have been working for 5, 10, 20, or 30 years has actually been in some form of pyramid scheme. To someone on the outside of the network marketing world, they would never understand the true meaning of a pyramid scheme other than what they have heard in the media. Once they have been exposed to the true meaning of a pyramid scheme and understand it in the network marketing world, they will look at it differently and realize that everyone is associated in some type of pyramid.

Chapter 5

Being Professional in Network Marketing

In any business, there is a level of professionalism that must be maintained in network marketing. Being professional can become a challenge. Professionalism is defined as "the conduct, aims, or qualities that characterize or mark a profession or a professional person ("Professionalism", Merriam-Webster Dictionary). Examples of professionalism consists of respect, good judgment, being polite, skillfulness, being well-trained, exercising good behavior, having a job well done, having a good work ethic, or being held accountable for your actions. These are all good traits to have in network marketing. However, there comes a time in your business where you will begin to see where you will see shifts in your business. The questions will begin to arise as to how you will handle it. That is when your professionalism comes in to play in this arena and it can either make your business or break your business.

A major part of your professionalism that will be tested is negativity. There will be times in your network marketing career that you will face some sort of negativity and unfortunately, a lot of it will come from fellow network marketers. For example, if you are having some success in your network marketing business and someone else is not having the same level of success, that person will experience some jealousy towards you and could try to hurt your business. This kind of jealousy can result into defamation of character against you or any other lie or rumor against you and your business.

Another example of negativity is someone new to the business being shown more attention than you. This can cause a lot of unnecessary problems. When you have someone new starting out in their business, they will receive additional attention but only to help that new representative start and grow their business. When someone who is not having success sees a new representative being shown more attention, once again you can find yourself facing defamation from the person. That person could find themselves quitting their business. When situations like this arises, do not allow yourself to "go to war" with that person. Be professional when situations like this arises and just simply do not respond to them at all. It will show that level of unprofessionalism when going to battle with someone quitting their business because someone is being shown more attention or because they were not having the same level of success. Remember, new people come into network marketing everyday just like you did when you first began so do not allow the other person to poison your mind or get involved in the politics.

In no way, shape or form should you let someone come in and try to steal your dream of having your own network marketing business away from you. Those are the people we call dream stealers. The dream stealers feel that since their dreams could not come true for whatever reason, your dreams of having your own network marketing business should not come true either. These people are the people that will tell you everything wrong about network marketing and they do not have a clue or have not done any research on network marketing. These are by far your biggest sceptics. Do not listen to them! If they knew about network marketing the way they say they do, they would have success.

The biggest negativity a network marketer will face is when they are introducing their business to someone new such as a potential business partner or customer is the word "no." Look, there are going to be plenty of people that will tell you "no." You have to be strong enough to take it and move on from the word "no." The people that will tell you "no" the most will be your friends and family. Most of your support for your network marketing business will come from strangers. The funny part is when you have strangers that will come in to your business and become either your new business partner or your customer, then your friends and family will eventually come around and they will become either a business partner or a customer. Most will become a customer.

Bottom line, learn how to absorb the word "no." Do not be afraid of the word. See the word as your best friend so when someone tells you no, you smile and say "thank you for listening and taking time out of your busy schedule and I hope you have a nice day." Say it with class, professionalism, and respect because down the line, that person will remember you and how respectful and professional you were and that can turn into a customer or a new business partner.

No matter who you encounter in your business, whether it is a friend, a family member, or a stranger, you must handle yourself in the most professional manner possible. Your professionalism speaks volumes. How you handle yourself with fellow business partners or customers will determine how successful your business will be in the long run. If for any reason it gets out that you were mean to a fellow network marketer, business partner, or a customer, your business will suffer. The biggest outlet people will find out about how you treated a fellow business partner, network marketer, or customer is social media. One person, one review can ruin your business and it can take months or years for you to recover. Be mindful of how you handle to everyone you come in contact with because everyone is watching you. Again, your professionalism is the key to your success in your network marketing business.

This can be the same when it comes to

building your team. If you are looking for new

representatives and you are recruiting them

the wrong way such as applying pressure to

that person to join your team or some form of

harassment, not only can it hurt your business,

it could get you in trouble with the company

that you are representing which could lead to

you being terminated. Do not allow these

practices to get in the way of your

professionalism. Remember, it is your face

that people see when it comes to your

business so again, professionalism is key in

network marketing.

Chapter 6

How to Handle Competition in Network Marketing

This is by far the most important chapter you will encounter in this book. Why is this the most important? Because not only are there many network marketing companies that exists but the competition between network marketing companies can get extremely ugly and can cause friction between fellow network marketers. The frictions that are caused can get so severe that it can cross the lines of defamation of character. In some cases, legal action has taken place for one reason or another. The competition can definitely test your professionalism. It will depend on how you handle the competition that will determine your success in network marketing so pay close attention to this chapter.

The first thing you are probably thinking is can the competition get this bad? The answer is yes! In some cases, you will have network marketing companies compete against each other just to see how big and bad they really are in the industry. In the beginning, you may look at it as friendly competition, but after being in the arena for a period of time, you begin to realize that it is not friendly competition, it is an outright fight for the top. But why all the bitterness? Why all of the competition? Why all of the fighting? Well, there may be many circumstances that may be taking place behind the scenes that you may not know about that are taking place that is causing the chaos.

The biggest chaos that is caused between network marketing companies is when someone in one network marketing company who is at the top of their game (probably one of the higher positioned people) leaves the company and goes to the other company and brings their team (fellow business partners) with them. When someone this huge in the company leaves for another company, they begin to call the other representatives from that company and tell them to join them. This is called cross-recruiting. This is a very unprofessional way of building your network marketing business. Cross-recruiting can come off as being desperate and it can eventually ruin your own network marketing business. Bottom line, do not cross-recruit! Many network marketing companies will sue other network marketing companies if they find out if cross-recruiting tactics are being used to get their representatives to join the competing network marketing companies. This is simply not necessary to do. If there are enough people leaving the company for any reason, it will begin to raise eyebrows. But it will be your decision whether or not to remain with the current network marketing company or not. Do not allow someone to pressure you to leave.

What to do if the current network marketing company that you are with ends up going out of business? If this happens, make sure that you are protected first and make sure that your team is protected as well. If you find out the right way ahead of time before the company closes its doors, make a smooth transition to another company. But before you make that transition, do your research on the new company that you are transitioning to before you make your move. Inform your up line of your move. Now note this, your up line will not like the fact that you will transition to another network marketing company. They will do everything in their power to keep you in that company until the very end because of their belief in the company. If your up line tells you anything similar in nature like that, they are not looking out for your best interest, they are looking out for their own interest and you need to protect yourself and your team's interest. Too many times will you find that a company is on the brink of financial ruin or closing their doors and instead of protecting their team, the up line will inform their team that everything is fine and you will continue to get paid and nothing has changed at all. Do not allow yourself to be fooled by your up line. Remember, this is your business, your hard work, your time and effort. The decision will be up to you if you want to stay with the company or transition to another network marketing company and continue to work hard for yourself and for your family and for your team.

Chapter 7

What Can We Learn About Network Marketing?

What can we learn about network marketing? Well, just like any industry, it has its ups and downs. In the beginning stages of your new network marketing business, you will start off slow just like anyone starting in any business. But as you continue to work hard and put in the hours and you begin to build a team of new business partners, your business will take off and you will begin to make money in this industry. Before doing all of this, you have to decide which network marketing company you would like to partner with.

Remember, there are many different

companies to choose from to be a part of in

the network marketing world. Do your

homework and choose wisely before you

decide on the right network marketing

company.

Be professional! Handle yourself with the

upmost professionalism in this network

marketing arena possible. Remember, when

you are presenting your business, you are the

face they see. With your face and your

character comes professionalism. Build a

strong team and you will have a strong

business. When your business and your team is strong, you will be a powerhouse to deal with in the network marketing industry. You will be the team to join, the person to talk to, and the ideal up line to work with. Again, with the professionalism that you will have, your team will develop the same professionalism and therefore, your team will be strong.

Be a leader and a student! Even though you are an up line to your team in your business, always stay in the learning mode and constantly stay in contact with your own up lines and continue to be the student of the network marketing industry. Even though you may be having success in your business, you can always continue to learn how you can fine tune some areas of your business to make it stronger. Never forget your humble beginnings. Do not forget that even though you are having success in network marketing, you had to start from somewhere. Do not turn your back on anyone that is trying to start out in network marketing. Remember, someone did not turn their backs on you so do not turn your back on anyone else.

Finally, make it fun! Network marketing is supposed to be fun and exciting. You are meeting new people and you are traveling and building your business and earning the money

that you deserve to earn. Network marketing

is about making it enjoyable and not about

being competitive and serious all the time.

When you're having fun, everyone else around

you is having fun. Make the best out of your

network marketing business, the network

marketing world and enjoy it with a smile.